The Japanese Table

SMALL PLATES FOR SIMPLE MEALS

To Yukiyo, who taught me these flavours.
To my parents, who taught me to cook.
To my sisters, without whose encouragement, eating
and enlightenment this would have remained scribbles
in a notebook.

The Japanese Table

SMALL PLATES FOR SIMPLE MEALS

SOFIA HELLSTEN

Design, words and photography

Hardie Grant

BOOKS

Contents

I've had a love story with Japan since my late teens and, athough I currently live in Stockholm, Sweden, I've tried to introduce ways of continuing to explore the edible treasures of the country, even when I'm not there. One such exploration is the local Japanese brunch experience *Leaves & Grains* I started a few years back. Another is this book, because – apart from funnelling my creativity into the kitchen – it allows me to indulge in my passions for photography and writing. So this is a compilation of all three elements: a profound fascination with Japanese food and culture as well as a fondness for standing in the kitchen and behind a camera. I have compiled all this into twelve chapters, each looking at a different element on my table.

The following pages are mainly about eating based on the *ichijuu-sansai* meal tradition – small plates for Japanese meals and having tea in the morning – and then, of course, some of my memories of Japan.

この本の事を考えはじめたのは約十年前。

大阪での一年間の留学を終え帰国した私は、だんだんと和食が恋しくなりました。

初めはなぜ留学先に日本を選んだのかも分からなかったけれど、日本での生活は驚きと発見の連続で 美しい文化も 独特の風習も 全て私の心に深く響きました。

記憶の中の和料理を少しずつ作りはじめ、心に残る感覚に近づけるよう、自分なりに何度も工夫を重ねました。日本から離れると無性に食べたくなる、西洋では出会えない味覚です。

日本では毎日当たり前のように食べていた食卓の味、日常の中の一汁三菜こそが私の中の和食。離れて気づいた和食への恋と、日本の思い出。

ソフィア

Preface

This book began taking shape about ten years ago, when I had just come back from living in Japan for a year. I didn't go for any particular reason, but somehow just ended up there. Ever since, I've been strangely attracted to that weird but wonderful place and what its beautiful culture has to offer. Back then I didn't know that I would write this book, but that's when I first began trying out dishes, tentatively recreating those flavours that I increasingly began to miss. I started serving Japanese dishes to my occasionally mesmerised, sometimes reluctant, but mainly excited family, scribbling down combinations of ingredients in a notebook.

The following pages present a collection of the dishes I miss the most when I'm not in Japan – the food I would have for breakfast or dinner at home. It is not the style you might be served at a Japanese restaurant in Stockholm, London or New York. Simply put, it is my interpretation of the Japanese home-cooked meal – or *ichijuu-sansai*.

When I was living in Osaka (or rather the very small city Kaizuka south thereof), my host mother, Yukiyo, would get up early every morning to prepare a rich miso soup, a small salad and grilled fish or an omelette for breakfast – along with rice, of course. Coming from a home where breakfast is sacred, I treasured these moments before running to Nishikinohama station to catch the train to school. It was Yukiyo who started teaching me to cook Japanese food in the first place. Everything she touches is as nourishing as it is flavoursome, so I watched her constantly, tasting carefully. And she was happy to answer my endless questions about ingredient measurements and weird vegetables.

I've thought long and hard about why the Japanese approach to food appeals to me. I grew up in a home where the vegetable was at the centre of the table and meat was a side dish; to use my mother's words: 'bacon is a spice'. It was also a home where fish was prominent and cream and butter were very, very rare. This meant that Japan and I were initially off to a good start.

Over the years, I have fallen more deeply in love with the way traditional Japanese cooking treats the ingredient like royalty – both in appearance and flavour. Spinach should taste like spinach at its finest. Sashimi is served with just soy sauce and wasabi for a reason – so that you can truly savour the flavour of the fish. These clean and simple flavours are still what makes me want to eat it every day.

Introduction

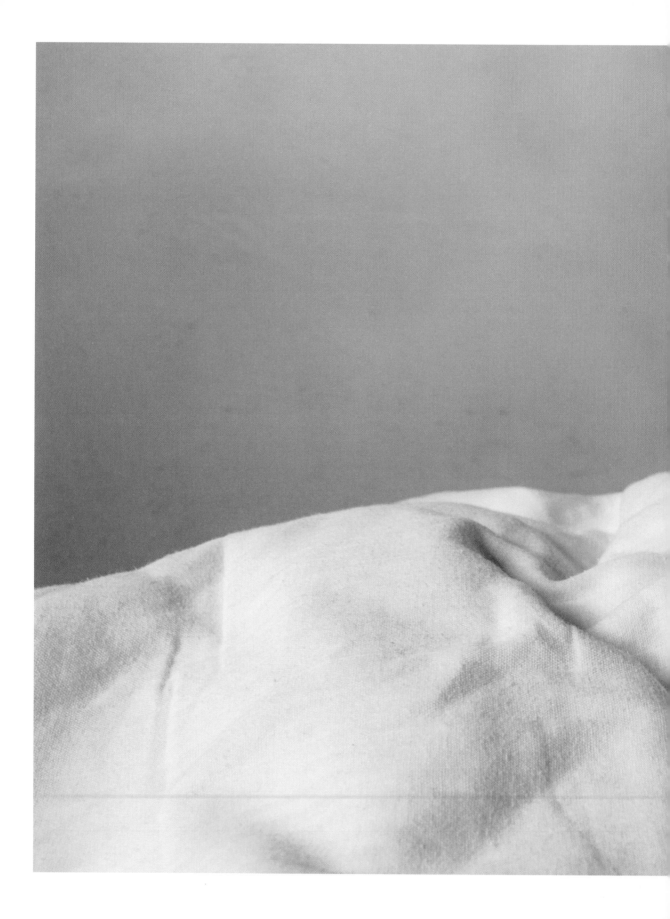

third side dish

main side dish

second side dish

tsukemono

rice

soup

In Japanese, *ichijuu-sansai* literally means 'one soup, three dishes'. It's a meal with its roots in Zen Buddhism, which has been the foundation of Japanese food culture since the Heian era in the 12th century. It is still what is served for breakfast or dinner in many Japanese homes and what I have chosen to use as a basis for this book.

The centrepiece of *ichijuu-sansai* is the essential steamed rice. This is accompanied by three side dishes (*okazu*) and one soup, as well pickles – *tsukemono*, as they're called in Japan. On most occasions, the side dishes include one main protein dish, such as grilled fish or tofu, and two smaller ones built around seasonal vegetables. The variations and combinations among side dishes are endless, ensuring that the meal satisfies all the senses and is a wonderful way of achieving diversity in your nourishment. Maybe that's where the beauty lies: in that the *ichijuu-sansai* gives you both variety and balance between different elements and flavours by preparing and presenting them in simple yet beautiful ways.

Recently, the *ichijuu-issai*, 'one soup, one dish', has been gaining popularity in Japan, since it's a simpler version requiring less time and preparation. Instead of abandoning the tradition altogether, people are just taking it down a notch. So if you feel intimidated, just start out small.

You can combine the dishes in this book as you like. Depending on mood and time, I go for just one side dish with rice and a soup, or full on with one protein-based main and two sides to go with it. Even just a rich soup with rice and pickles will do the trick. Towards the end of the book, you'll find some of my favourite combinations.

Ichijuu-sansai

The intention behind this book is not to account for a range of traditional Japanese dishes and their exact make-up. The dishes I have chosen are simply flavours I've stumbled upon or grown to love, and have created and recreated. It is food that I regularly make in my own kitchen, with roots in Japanese homecooking and their way of building a meal. The dishes are all uncomplicated, both in flavour and in preparation, letting each ingredient speak for itself.

Many of these side dishes can be prepared and put in the refrigerator until you are ready to serve, then you just need to heat up some soup, boil the rice and choose which dish to put on which plate. It takes no longer than making a proper avocado sandwich or preparing a bowl of pasta.

As much as I wanted to share what I love in terms of the flavours of Japanese food, this book is also an invitation to cook Japanese dishes without making it complicated. Simplicity is the keyword here. I hope that these are recipes that you dare to try out on any ordinary Tuesday or Friday. For this reason, you won't find very complex and lengthy guides to making the perfect fish stock for miso soup, or pickles that need to be stored for months before eating. I use shop-bought stock base for my miso soup and am far too impatient to wait more than a day or two for my pickles.

The bottom line is that it's not difficult. You don't need a cabinet full of spices or an arsenal of peculiar equipment. Nine times out of ten, a good knife, a saucepan and a frying pan (skillet) should be all the equipment you need, along with some miso, dashi, soy sauce and mirin.

I've selected lighter dishes, which, in combination, make for great dinners or kick-ass bento lunches. And if you're like me and want a substantial meal for breakfast, they are all perfect for that too.

First taste

In the cupboard

The must-have ingredients

BONITO FLAKES

These are ultra-thin flakes of *katsuobushi* (dried, fermented and smoked skipjack tuna), one of the main ingredients for a traditional dashi. In addition to this, bonito flakes are frequently used as a topping for different dishes, to give an extra injection of umami and to enhance the presentation of the dish. When sprinkled on hot dishes, the thin flakes 'dance' from the heat waves rising from the hot food.

DASHI POWDER

Dashi is the Japanese word for stock. The powdered version, often fish-based, is an oh-so-versatile basis for stock, which you simply mix with hot water. Dashi is probably more important than salt when it comes to Japanese cooking. It's a foundation for building flavour in just about everything. I mainly use the variant made from the fish bonito, which has a nice smoky note to it, and the algae *konbu*. Throughout the book, I will refer to water mixed with dashi powder simply as 'dashi'.

IRIGOMA

Irigoma is basically just toasted sesame seeds, though in my opinion *irigoma* is different from the sesame seeds you get at a regular supermarket, with both more flavour and fragrance. Even though *irigoma* can be replaced by unhulled sesame seeds that you toast yourself, I highly recommend buying the real deal if you can find it at your Asian market.

SOY SAUCE

Soy sauce also goes under the name *shoyu*, and is also commonly known through the brand Kikkoman. Japanese soy sauce differs from Chinese soy sauce in being brewed with 50 per cent wheat in addition to the soy beans, giving it a slightly sweeter, less sharp flavour. *Shoyu* comes in two main variants: the dark *koikuchi* and the lighter *usukuchi*. The dark version can easily be found in any supermarket and will be fine for all these recipes. However, if you can get hold of good-quality light soy sauce, it's totally worth it.

MIRIN

This Japanese low-alcohol cooking rice wine works both as a sweetener and gives a little acidity to a dish.

MISO

Miso is a thick paste made from fermenting soy beans with salt and *koji* (the fungus *Aspergillus oryzae*). There is a range of variations where, for example, rice, barley or soy sauce are mixed in with the beans, giving rise to a variety of shades from reddish brown and almost black to a yellow-white, depending on the ingredients and the degree of fermentation. Miso is a fundamental ingredient in the Japanese kitchen, used daily not just for miso soup, but also for pickling vegetables or making dressings and marinades. Apart from being an explosion of umami, it is high in proteins, minerals and vitamins, as well as contributing a sizeable dose of necessary nutrients and probiotics. A useful tip is to store opened miso in an airtight container in the freezer – that way it keeps for much longer (and since it doesn't freeze solid, it's still easy to spoon out the amount you need).

NORI

An edible seaweed dried into sheet form, nori is mainly used for wrapping sushi or *onigiri* (page 29), but is also frequently used for garnishing and to add extra flavour.

VINEGAR

I use either rice vinegar (a must-have when making sushi) or grain vinegar (a staple for dressings). Rice vinegar is not as sharp in flavour as a cider vinegar, but is a little more acidic than grain vinegar, which has a subtle bran flavour.

SAKE

This Japanese rice brew is a great sweetener and fantastic for both marinades or boiled dishes. If I don't finish off a whole bottle, I freeze what's left in ice-cube trays to have portion-sized quantities to use for future cooking.

VEGETABLE OIL

Any flavourless vegetable oil, such as sunflower, rapeseed (canola) or high-grade white sesame oil works.

IRIKO

Iriko are dried anchovies. These little fish can be a bit hard to find but, if you can locate them, they make a great stock together with a piece of *konbu*.

KONBU

An edible kelp, or seaweed, commonly used for making dashi, *konbu* is bought in the form of dark greenish sheets, which soften when put into water.

USUKUCHI SOY SAUCE

The dark soy sauce is great for making sauces or salty stocks, but when cooking lighter dishes with bright colours, *usukuchi*, the lighter version, is preferable since it is both less salty and doesn't brown the dish to the same extent as the darker *koikuchi*.

PONZU

Ponzu is a tart, citrus-flavoured sauce, not far from a vinaigrette, which is used for everything from sashimi to hot simmered pot dishes. I often use it on a salad as it is or as part of a dressing. Yuzu *ponzu* is a favourite.

SHICHIMI

Shichimi, meaning 'seven flavours', is a Japanese spice mix containing, of course, seven different spices: coarsely ground red chilli pepper (the main ingredient), ground *sanshō* (Japanese pepper), roasted orange peel, black sesame seed, white sesame seed, hemp seed, ground ginger, nori or aonori (both of which are types of seaweed). It is often used for noodle soups or to season rice crackers.

YUZU JUICE

One perk of living in Japan (and there are many when it comes to food) is the number of different citrus fruits you can buy. One of the more commonly used ones is the yuzu – which looks like a lime-sized grapefruit and tastes similar – often used like lemons are used in other cuisines. As the fresh fruits are not always easy to find outside Japan, you can get bottled yuzu juice to add that tart flavour.

KNIVES

I usually opt for one large, very sharp knife. As I mostly chop vegetables, I choose accordingly.

MANDOLINE

You'll love a mandoline, and love yourself for buying one. Leafy thin slices of vegetables will magically appear before your eyes. But don't be too hasty – fingers are at risk.

TAMAGOYAKI PAN

If you really want to go for it you can get yourself a rectangular frying pan for making perfect Japanese omelettes (page 58). It makes rolling that egg a whole lot easier, although I have to admit it might be going a bit too far.

HEAVY-BASED SAUCEPAN

For boiling rice and making soups, use a good-quality saucepan with a heavy base.

GLASS JARS

A selection of glass jars will be useful for storing pickled greens, miso or prepared side dishes.

CHOPSTICKS

If you want to brag about your chopstick skills, I can recommend using the longer cooking chopsticks, *saibashi*, although they're not essential. Nevertheless, I suggest you pick up a pair of regular chopsticks to use when serving as they make it a lot easier to arrange the food beautifully. And then you need some for eating, of course.

PORCELAIN AND CERAMICS

Make sure that each person has a bowl for rice and one for soup. Apart from that, either plate everything on one plate, or individually in a range of smaller plates and bowls. Remember, the visual presentation is just as much part of the experience as the flavour, so don't forget to spend some time on making your food look – as well as taste – beautiful.

I remember the day I fully realised what rice was all about. I was visiting a small neighbourhood restaurant south of Osaka, a place only the workers in the area frequent and where the median age is probably around 70. It's all concrete floors and metal trays (though not in the hip Brooklyn way) but with an 84-year-old *ojiisan* (grandpa) who really knows what he is doing. The rice grains there shine like silver, have the perfect chewiness and just the right amount of sweet notes. No wonder people call it the Silver Rice restaurant. Once you have experienced that, you just have to keep eating properly cooked rice. There's no going back.

Nowadays, one of the best smells I know is the moment, early in the morning, when the lid is lifted from a pan of freshly steamed rice. In the same way that waking up to a freshly baked loaf of bread fills your heart; it brings about the equivalent feeling of caring nourishment. Biting into a savoury *onigiri* (rice ball) or sweet *mochi* (rice cake) never ceases to leave me touched. How can such a seemingly simple ingredient have so much depth and versatility?

When I talk about rice from here onwards, I am referring to the short-grain Japonica rice, which is the type of rice widely used in Japan. Of course, the varieties within this category are endless, but that's another book entirely.

Rice

Gohan

The bowl of white rice. In Japanese it is called *gohan*, which is the same word as the one for meal or food. The essentiality. The part that is supposed to fill you up and balance out the flavours of the surrounding dishes. A meal is rarely complete without it. Excluding it would be like serving a Swede pickled herring without potatoes. Still, it's a food that, until recently, has been much overlooked beyond eastern latitudes.

People often get scared away from boiling rice after having failed once too often. In Japan, almost everyone owns a state-of-the-art rice cooker, engineered to perfection, so you rarely need to do more than wash the grains. If you are super-hipster, or very traditional, you steam it in a *donabe* (clay pot) over a fire, although even for most Japanese people that is taking it too far. All the same, serving a *chawan* (rice bowl) filled with glittering rice without rice cookers or heavy ceramics is not impossible; it just requires a little patience. Washing, waiting, boiling and waiting again.

Serves 4

200 ml (7 fl oz/1 cup) rice*
300 ml (10 fl oz/1¼ cups) water

** use short-grain Japonica rice
(such as Yumepirika or Koshi-Hikari,
available from Asian stores)*

STEP 1
Measure the rice by volume. Wash the rice in cold water until the water is more or less clear. This is to wash away the surface starch and give you the right amount of stickiness when steamed.

STEP 2
Drain the rice and put it in a heavy-based saucepan with a lid, pour in the measured water and let the rice soak for at least 45 minutes, preferably 1 hour. This is to allow the grains to start absorbing water, which helps you avoid a mushy exterior and a hard core after steaming.

STEP 3
After soaking, put the saucepan over a high heat and bring to a fast boil. Once boiling, immediately lower the temperature to almost a simmer. Continue to cook at a gentle simmer with the lid on for 12 minutes, then remove from the heat.

STEP 4
Let the rice sit in the pan, away from the heat, for about 10 minutes without removing the lid. This is to let the steam be absorbed into the grains before serving.

Don't be impatient and skip any of the steps – they are all equally essential and the result will be well worth the wait.

Zosui

This is a warm and soft dish, perfect for cold winter days or when you need something comforting that is ready in a moment. *Zosui* is made from steamed rice, water and dashi – it's a savoury rice porridge that comes in a range of variations with different toppings and flavours. It has a sibling called *okayu* – made from just plain water and rice – but I prefer the added saltiness from the dashi and the fact that I can use pre-steamed rice. Usually I steam more rice than I need, wrap it up in portion sizes and put it in the freezer. That way you can have a delicious meal on the table in minutes, regardless of your level of energy or timeframe.

Serves 1

150 ml (5 fl oz/scant ⅔ cup) water
½ teaspoon dashi powder
¼ recipe quantity freshly steamed rice (page 22)
1 egg
1 spring onion (scallion), chopped (or use ramsons or Asian chives)
salt or soy sauce, preferably light
shichimi or nori, for topping
tsukemono (page 45–55), to serve

Bring the water and dashi powder to the boil in a saucepan. Taste the dashi to get the right amount of saltiness – it should be just a little on the salty side as you can always adjust with salt or soy sauce towards the end. Add the rice, lower the heat and let it simmer for 1–2 minutes, uncovered.

Whisk the egg in a separate bowl, then add to the pan with the spring onion, stirring continuously. Keep stirring over a low heat for a minute or so until the egg starts to coagulate but the porridge remains creamy.

Remove from the heat, taste and add soy sauce or salt, if needed. Serve topped with *shichimi* and/or nori and a side of *tsukemono*.

Onigiri

Onigiri literally means 'handful'. A handful of rice – or a rice ball if you will – but a handful of rice sounds nicer in my opinion. It stems from a solution to the problem of how to conveniently bring food along for travelling: filling a handful of rice with something savoury, squeezing it tight and wrapping it in seaweed.

If you have ever visited Japan, you know that there is a convenience store on every corner, no matter how far out in the middle of nowhere you are. Much can be said about the food available in such places but the *onigiri* shelf is no joke. It's a life-saver. Especially if you have missed breakfast, or need a second one to avoid the 11 o'clock dip. The same goes for these three simple variations.

Serves 4

RICE
1 recipe quantity freshly steamed rice (page 22)
salt
nori for wrapping (optional)

BONITO
2 large pinches of bonito flakes
a dash of soy sauce

NORI-SESAME
1–2 sheets of nori, cut into strips
1 teaspoon irigoma, or toasted sesame seeds

TUNA-MAYO
200 g (7 oz) tin of tuna in oil, drained
1 tablespoon mayonnaise
1 teaspoon wasabi

Set the cooked rice aside to cool while preparing the fillings.

MAKING THE FILLINGS
For the bonito filling, mix the bonito flakes and soy sauce; it should bind together a little. Nori-sesame just requires you to mix the rice with the nori and sesame seeds. For the tuna-mayo, mix the fish with the mayonnaise and wasabi. Taste and adjust the level of spiciness.

SHAPING THE ONIGIRI
When your filling is ready, put a little salt in a bowl of water. This is for dampening your hands so that the rice doesn't stick to them when squeezing the balls together. Wet your hands in the water, then take a handful of rice and push the filling into the middle before folding over the edges to enclose the filling. Squeeze the rice into a round or triangular shape, then wrap the finished ball in nori sheets, if you wish.

Your hand size determines how big you make the onigiri, and if you're lucky it relates to how hungry you are. If you feel the mixture is getting too sticky, use a piece of cling film (plastic wrap) between your hand and the rice while you shape the balls.

The soup is the *juu* in the *ichijuu-sansai*. A warm bowl of wonderful umami. Though it's hardly ever eaten on its own, it is an essential part of the meal. Whenever you get plain rice in Japan, a bowl of soup comes as a side. The exceptions are dishes such as *ocha-tsuke* – rice with different flavourings, soaked in green tea; *okayu* – plain rice porridge; or *zosui* (page 26), where liquid is already added to the rice.

The most common version of soup is the miso soup, which sometimes has a bad reputation outside of Japan – probably because people have encountered numerous examples prepared without love and put on a heater for far too long in various third-grade sushi establishments in suburbs around the world. In reality, a simple miso soup is almost impossible to mess up.

Soup

Simple miso soup

My Japanese host mother, Yukiyo, still makes the best miso soup I've ever tasted – always perfectly balanced in saltiness and depth. It might be the one thing that I most look forward to eating whenever I go to Osaka. Always served with a few well chosen and perfectly cooked vegetables or proteins. Always second helpings.

Made from a base of dashi and soy sauce, to which you add miso along with a few pieces of vegetables or protein – the variations have no end to them. Spring onion (scallion), wakame and tofu. Onion and potato. Daikon and heart clams or cockles. Usually I just throw in whatever I have in the refrigerator at the time. As for how many additions you should add to your soup. Well, that depends on how hungry you are. Let's say at least two shiitake per person. And one onion should cover four portions in combination with other greens. I try not to make rules here.

Serves 4

DASHI
1 litre (34 fl oz/4 cups) water
2 teaspoons dashi powder
2 tablespoons brown miso paste
2 teaspoons soy sauce

ADDITION VARIATIONS
tofu, spring onions (scallions)
and wakame
sliced carrots, fried tofu and spring
onions (scallions)
1 onion and 2 potatoes, sliced
a few shiitake mushrooms and spring
onion (scallion)
heart clams or cockles, daikon
and enoki mushrooms
½ aubergine (eggplant), sliced
2 shallots

For the additions, choose one of the variations suggested here, or use whatever you have available.

To make the dashi, bring the water and dashi powder to a gentle boil in a large saucepan over a medium heat. Add any hard vegetables, tofu or seafood that you have chosen to use and simmer until they are tender. Lower the heat.

Scoop up some miso with a ladle and add it to the soup by mixing it with a little bit of dashi at a time in the ladle to liquefy the paste. Once you have a smooth base, add any tender greens and let them soften. Taste for saltiness and add a dash of soy sauce or water, if needed. Serve warm.

The saltiness of different miso pastes vary, so exactly how much soy sauce you need will differ depending on this. Remember not to boil the soup after the miso has been added as this will destroy both flavour and the probiotics that are a result of the miso's fermentation process. Just heat gently instead. If you make a vegetarian version of the soup, it keeps overnight on the counter and you can easily heat it up for breakfast.

Clear shiitake soup

This is a lighter alternative to the more hearty miso soup. Basically a dashi made from *konbu*, shiitake mushrooms and *iriko* (dried anchovies), topped with some fresh mushrooms and garlicky ramsons or Asian chives. Subtle flavours but satisfying and very beautiful to serve. The only catch is to remember to prepare it a day in advance.

Serves 4

DASHI
1 litre (34 fl oz/4 cups) water
2 × 8 cm (¾ × 3½ in) piece of konbu
15 iriko (dried anchovies)
10 small shiitake mushrooms

FOR SERVING
about 15 leaves of ramson
or Asian chives
½–1 teaspoon salt
1 tablespoon soy sauce
about 12 small shiitake mushrooms

PREPARING THE DASHI
Put everything into a large saucepan and bring to a gentle boil, lifting off any foam that rises to the surface with a slotted spoon. Let it simmer gently for a few minutes. Turn off the heat and leave it to cool down before putting it in the refrigerator overnight (note that all the ingredients should be left in the liquid).

BEFORE SERVING
Pour the dashi through a sieve (fine-mesh strainer) and then gently heat it up along with a few leaves of ramsons or Asian chives (reserving a few for garnish). Make sure not to boil the soup at this point, as this will cause the dashi to lose flavour. Add salt and soy sauce until you have reached a nice balance, which is when the flavours really come out. When you've reached desired saltiness, remove the leaves. Add the mushrooms and simmer for about 5 minutes until soft. Just before serving, add the remaining ramsons or Asian chives.

Daikon with white miso & yuzu

A few years ago, I was invited to a culinary event in Tokyo that was wholly dedicated to the Japanese Buddhist cuisine *shōjin ryōri*, a type of vegan food usually served at temples around the country. It is a way of cooking that reduces waste to an absolute minimum, while the seasoning of dishes is achieved using only products from the vegetable world. During the event, a prominent Kyoto chef cooked a simple vegetable dashi based on the principles of *shōjin ryōri*. While tasting it, I was stunned to silence – never had I imagined that just a selection of vegetables could bring out such depth of flavour. This recipe came about in a pursuit to explore *shōjin ryōri* a little further, placing one of my favourite vegetables, daikon, at the centre and then dressing it with a sweet miso. It is a thick, creamy soup, which requires a little more effort and preparation in advance, but the result is beautiful. Placing it on the table almost feels like giving someone a small present with a citrusy perfume.

Serves 4

8 cm (3½ in) piece of daikon
4 cm (1½ in) piece of konbu
200–300 ml (7–10 fl oz/ scant 1–1¼ cup) water
2 tablespoons white miso paste
sea salt, to taste
1½ teaspoons soy sauce
2 tablespoons mirin
yuzu or lemon zest

PREPARING THE DASHI

Wash and peel the daikon, then cut it into four 2-cm (¾-in) thick slices. Put the daikon, cut-side down, in a heavy-based pan with the *konbu*. Add enough of the water just to reach the top of the daikon. Bring slowly to the boil, then reduce the heat and simmer for 30 minutes. Add a little more hot water as it evaporates – the water line should never go below half of the daikon's thickness.

When the daikon no longer has a white core, and it slides easily off a thin skewer, remove from the heat and add enough water so that it just covers the daikon. Leave the daikon and *konbu* in the liquid, cover and leave to cool at room temperature, preferably overnight.

BEFORE SERVING

Take out the daikon and set aside. Remove the *konbu*. Slowly heat up the stock, being careful not to let it boil, stir in the miso and mix until smooth. Carefully season with salt and soy sauce. Add the daikon used for making the stock back in and warm over a low heat, making sure not to boil. Place one piece of daikon in each soup bowl, pour over the soup, then garnish with the yuzu/lemon zest for fragrance.

The daikon is left in the water to cool in order to take up the konbu flavour from the water and vice versa, so that time overnight is worth it. I prefer to use a sweeter white miso for the best result.

One of my favourite pastimes while living in Kyoto was walking around the heart of the city, passing stores filled with barrel after barrel packed with wondrous *tsukemono*, Japanese pickles. I was humbled by the the care and effort that goes into making that small pickle which elevates any meal.

Originally, like so many other foods, *tsukemono* was a way of preserving summer greens into the winter months, with the positive side effect of the healthy microbes that come from fermentation. The literal translation of the word is 'pickled thing' and these things can be pickled in everything from salt, sugar or vinegar to rice bran, mustard or miso, to name just a few. *Tsukemono* come in an endless variety of shapes, colours and flavours. The appeal is no less visual than in taste. Commonly eaten together with your everyday bowl of rice, *tsukemono* also go very well as snacks with a drink or as a garnish for a meal, brightening up the plates with their fragrance and colour. No wonder they also go under the names *konomono* (香の物), *oshinko* (御新香) or *okōko* (御香々), all meaning 'fragrant dish'.

In modern Japan it is becoming increasingly uncommon to make your own *tsukemono*, however it is not as hard as it sounds, and keeping a jar or two of *tsukemono* in the refrigerator is an excellent way of adding some spark to any meal. The following recipes are interpretations of the *asazuke*, quick pickles that don't require big barrels or months of fermentation: you'll have them on the table the next day.

Tsukemono

Miso-pickled radish

The bright pink radish with dark green leaves is like a delicate painting, and the salty miso, together with the already peppery radish, creates a unique flavour. The first time I made this, it was a revelation and now it is a long-time favourite among friends and family. The best part? You only need two ingredients.

Serves 4

about 10 radishes with leaves
250 g (9 oz) brown miso paste

Start by washing the radishes thoroughly. Put them in a bowl of cold water, rinse them well, then change the water, repeating until all the soil and dirt have gone. Shake off in a strainer and then pat dry using paper towels. It is important that the radishes and leaves are both dry and clean.

In a clean glass jar, layer the miso and whole radishes. Make sure the miso covers all of the greens. Seal the jar tightly, then put in the refrigerator for 1–2 days before eating.

When you are ready to eat them, take as many radishes as you need out of the miso and wash away the miso under cold running water.

The radishes keep in the miso for about 7 days. The longer you leave them, the saltier they'll become.

I always re-use the remaining miso a second time, straight after I've finished off the first batch (they are usually gone in moments), either for a few more radishes or for tender spring carrots. Just follow the same procedure.

Shiso- & salt-pickled cucumber

A favourite in the summer when the smaller cucumbers are fresh, this *tsukemono* has a perfect cooling saltiness to contrast with sweet rice or mild noodles. This also makes a great topping to any fresh salad, or just serve it with mozzarella and olive oil. The shiso gives a nice contrast to the gentle cucumber flavour. However, you can omit the shiso if you can't find it.

Serves 4–6

1 small cucumber or ½ large one, about 200 g (7 oz)
2 shiso leaves (optional)
1 teaspoon salt

Wash the cucumber and shiso leaves, if using, then pat dry. Using a mandoline or a very sharp knife, slice the cucumber into 1–2 mm (1/16 in) thin slices. Cut the shiso first into thin strips, then again in the other direction into smaller pieces. Mix the cucumber, shiso and salt and put in a plastic bag. Press out the air and close tightly. Put the bag under pressure in a container and leave to stand in the refrigerator for 1–2 days before eating. It will keep for up to a week in the refrigerator.

The smaller new cucumbers give the best result, so make sure you try this when they are in season. Also, if you like a crunchier pickle, you can cut the cucumber into small chunks instead of thin slices, as this will keep the texture firmer.

432円
432円
540円
540円

756円
756円
756円

648円

頂きます

Ginger-pickled Chinese leaf

You've probably come across kimchi a few times – that funky, spicy Korean lacto-fermented cabbage? I really like kimchi but, in combination with the more subtle Japanese flavours, it's not a perfect match. In my quest to find that same funkiness that comes from lacto-fermenting cabbage, but with notes better suited to the Japanese palate, I ended up seasoning Chinese leaves (napa cabbage) with smoky bonito and the spiciness of ginger. It turned out to be a keeper.

Serves 10

½ head of Chinese leaves (napa cabbage)
3 cm (1¼ in) fresh ginger root,
peeled and cut into thin slices
2–3 teaspoons salt (adjust to about
2–3% of the weight of the vegetable)
1 tablespoon bonito flakes

Cut off a very thin part from the bottom of the cabbage (the leaves should still hold together) and then split lengthways down the middle. Rinse thoroughly under running water, remove any outer leaves that don't look perfect and shake off any excess water.

With clean hands, spread the ginger, salt and bonito flakes in between the cabbage leaves so that all areas are covered. Make sure you massage thoroughly and don't miss the gaps close to the bottom of the cabbage. Put the leaves in a plastic bag. Press out the air and close tightly. Put the bag under something heavy in a container and leave to stand in the refrigerator for 1–2 days before eating – you can easily tell when the cabbage has started to release liquid.

When you are ready to serve, take the container out of the refrigerator and cut off as much as you need in smaller pieces, returning the rest to the refrigerator. It will keep for up to a week in the refrigerator.

A plastic container filled with stones makes a good weight to keep the pickle under the liquid, or you can use tins. Don't forget to eat the ginger as well!

When it comes to eggs, Japan has won me over. I was never a big fan as a child, but how the Japanese prepare these oval delights opened up a new world for me. Everything from pickled egg yolks and *onsen tamago* to the sweet *datemaki* – New Year's omelette with fish cake. In Japan, an egg is not just an egg; it can take so many different forms and shapes, and that is maybe what I've grown to like about it. Here are just a few of the most classic preparations, which will most definitely get you through the day beautifully.

Egg

Tamagoyaki

Fluffy, soft and with a touch of saltiness, this omelette is just as perfect for breakfast as it is for lunch or dinner. Just as good scrambled eggs needs a certain degree of care, so does this. It can seem tricky at first, but there's no need to set the bar too high; a few times in the pan and you'll get the hang of it. Trust me, it's worth two or three failures. The original shape of the *tamagoyaki* requires a special, rectangular frying pan (page 17), which is not a common thing to have at home unless you are Japanese. A small frying pan (skillet) should work, even if it makes the rolling part a little bit trickier. It will also mean you won't be able to get the traditional shape, but the flavour will still be splendid.

Serves 4

3 eggs
1½ tablespoons water
½ teaspoon dashi powder
¾ teaspoon soy sauce, light if available,
plus extra for serving
a handful of flat-leaf parsley
(optional), chopped
1 spring onion (scallion), sliced
(optional), plus 1, sliced, to garnish
vegetable oil, for frying

Crack the eggs into a bowl, add the water, dashi powder and soy sauce and whisk together. Add the parsley and spring onion (scallion), if using.

Heat a small frying pan (skillet) – or a rectangular pan, if you have one – to medium–high heat and add a splash of oil (don't be too shy with this). Pour a quarter of the egg mixture into the pan and roll the pan around so that it's evenly spread out. Leave to cook until the egg sheet has almost coagulated.

Now start the rolling process. Using a broad, thin spatula, fold over a small part of the egg and then roll the 'sheet' into a small roll. Push to the opposite end of the pan, add more oil if the pan is dry, then add another quarter of the egg mixture. Lift the roll so that the new egg mixture flows under and glues together the old and new egg. When nearly coagulated, start rolling again, so that the new egg rolls around the old. When that is all rolled up, push it to the other side of the pan and start the procedure again. Keep going until all the egg mixture is finished. Remove the roll from the frying pan and let it rest for a few minutes before cutting. Serve with a dash of soy sauce and a few slices of spring onion.

Soy-pickled eggs

These are usually something you might come across as a topping on a ramen. In my opinion, they also serve as a fantastic side to rice, with both some acidity and saltiness in combination with the fatty creaminess of the egg yolk. It's also one of the quickest side dishes you can have in your refrigerator.

Serves 4

4 eggs
6 tablespoons soy sauce
5 tablespoons rice vinegar
4 tablespoons mirin

Take the eggs out of the refrigerator to let them come to room temperature. Bring a large saucepan of water to the boil, then reduce to a medium–high heat and carefully lower the eggs into the water using a spoon (this way they won't crack from hitting the bottom). Boil for exactly 6 minutes and 30 seconds (7 minutes if the eggs are large, or used directly from the refrigerator).

When the time is up, immediately transfer the eggs into a bowl of cold water and leave to rest until cool. Peel the eggs and place in a clean glass jar together with the rest of the ingredients, making sure the eggs are completely covered by the liquid. Leave to stand in the refrigerator for at least 12 hours; they are probably best after about 24 hours.

When serving, simply cut an egg in half. They keep for about 3 days in the refrigerator.

Tamago-sando with miso mayonnaise

Tamago-sando, or egg sandwich, might sound plain, on the verge of boring and also not very Japanese. Well, let's put it like this: the best egg sandwich I've had in my entire life was in a small coffee parlour in the basement of a dull 1970s Ginza building. The egg was incredibly light and fluffy, contrasting beautifully with the soft toasted bread, crispy salad and smooth mayonnaise. A great cup of pour-over coffee (a method with Japanese origin, where the hot water is poured over freshly ground beans by hand) on the side and my day was made. This is an interpretation of that experience.

Serves 1

FILLING
1 tablespoon mayonnaise
½ teaspooon white sweet miso

OMELETTE
2 eggs
2 tablespoons water
⅓ teaspoon dashi powder
1 tablespoon butter

TO SERVE
2 slices of white bread
1 leaf of crispy lettuce, cut in half

Start by mixing the mayonnaise with the miso and set aside.

Cut the crusts off the bread and rinse the lettuce in cold water. Set aside while you cook the egg.

Whisk together eggs, water and dashi powder in a bowl. Heat a frying pan (skillet) over a low heat, add the butter and leave it to melt, then pour in the egg mixture. Let the egg set a little, then push the edges in towards the middle and tilt the pan so that the liquid spreads evenly over the base of the pan. Repeat until the egg is almost set, then fold the sides gently towards the middle so that you get a squarish shape. Turn the omelette over and fry swiftly on the other side. Set aside on a plate.

Toast the bread lightly and spread the mayonnaise on both pieces of bread. Place the lettuce on the bread and put the egg in the middle. Cut in half and serve with a good cup of pour over coffee.

If you buy mayonnaise, I highly recommend the Japanese Kewpie. I can't really explain why, but the flavour is really something different from your regular store-bought mayonnaise. You will want to put it on everything, I promise. In order to get the proper taste of a Japanese tamago sandwich I propose you use a white bread that is slightly sweet.

Seasonality is an essential element in the Japanese kitchen. Enjoying the flavour of an ingredient when it is at its peak, while taking advantage of what is most bounteous in nature at any given moment, is inherent in the food culture. The name for this seasonality of food is 'shun' (旬) and the dishes are created and composed to follow nature's changes throughout the year, using the tender greens, shoots and flowers of the spring and summer as well as the roots and foliage of the autumn (fall) and winter. So don't feel obliged to stick to the greens I've used here, try using whatever is freshest and most abundant on any given day.

Greens

Spinach ohitashi with shiitake

Spinach *ohitashi* is a standard at the Japanese table and is almost impossible to mess up. *Ohitashi* means 'to steep vegetables in a dashi-based sauce', so basically this is spinach with an umami-packed sauce. It's a light, healthy dish, which I tend to return to again and again. It's also a great dish to make ahead, as the greens benefit from soaking in the dashi.

Serves 4

VEGETABLES
4 shiitake mushrooms, about 25 g (1 oz)
500 g (1 lb 2 oz) spinach, baby or regular

DASHI
100 ml (3½ fl oz/scant ½ cup) water
2 tablespoons sake
4 tablespoons mirin
1 teaspoon dashi powder
2½ tablespoons soy sauce

TO SERVE
violets (or other edible flowers when in season)
irigoma, or toasted sesame seeds (optional)

Clean any dirt off the shiitake mushrooms using paper towels, then cut into small pieces.

Bring the water for the dashi to the boil in a saucepan, then blanch the mushrooms for 45 seconds. Lift them out of the water and rinse under cold running water until cold. Be sure to keep the blanching water.

Add the dashi ingredients to the reserved water and bring to a gentle boil, then set aside to cool.

Bring another large saucepan of water to the boil while you wash and trim the spinach. If you are using violets, blanch them in the water for about 15 seconds, then take out and rinse in cold water. Put the spinach into the same boiling water and blanch for about 40 seconds. Remove and quickly rinse in cold water until completely cool. Use your hands to squeeze out any excess water from the spinach. If using regular spinach, cut the leaves into 4 cm (1½ in) pieces.

Mix the greens with the dashi and set aside to soak in the liquid for at least an hour. They will keep in the refrigerator for up to 3 days.

When ready to serve, arrange the vegetables in four small bowls and top with either blanched flowers or toasted, lightly ground sesame seeds.

If you are in a hurry, it's okay to substitute the dashi with a splash of good-quality soy sauce.

Simple wafuu salad

This salad is almost too easy, but sometimes easy is perfect. I make it in different variations depending on what's in my refrigerator or in season. Even so, the shiso version is a favourite because of the combination with the peppery notes from the radish. The tanginess from the ponzu also works as a great substitute for *tsukemono* if you don't have any of those at hand.

Serves 4

SHISO VERSION
½ daikon
4 radishes
1 small silver onion
2 shiso leaves
½ sheet nori, cut into strips,
or 3–4 pinches of pre-cut strips

FENNEL VERSION
¼ daikon
1 fennel bulb
a small bunch of dill or shiso
zest of 1 lemon

DRESSING
1–2 tablespoons ponzu
or
2 tablespoons rice vinegar mixed
with 1 tablespoon soy sauce

Wash, peel and slice the vegetables thinly using a mandoline. If you are using the onion, let it rest in cold water for a while to remove the sharpness. Wash and roughly chop any herbs (shiso or dill).

Arrange everything on a plate, pour over the dressing and top with lemon zest or nori.

Slice some extra vegetables while you're at it, then all you have to do is pour dressing over them for your next meal.

Miso & yuzu aubergine

When I first returned from Japan, one of the dishes I started experimenting with was *nasu dengaku*: aubergine covered with sweet white miso, which is then baked or grilled. I would always order this dish whenever I went to an *izakaya* or a small restaurant, because who doesn't want to have the best of both worlds: umami-packed miso and smooth aubergine (eggplant)? Later on I realised it runs in the family; when I make dinner for my younger sister she always begs me to make *nasu dengaku*. This recipe is a twist on the more traditional version, made in a pan instead of the oven and with acidity from the yuzu and peppery notes from the mustard in addition to the sweet white miso. A pretty great combination, if you ask me.

Serves 4

1 medium-sized aubergine (eggplant)
1 yuzu
3 tablespoons white sweet miso
2 tablespoons sake
2 tablespoons sugar
2 teaspoons soy sauce
1 teaspoon Dijon mustard
4–5 tablespoons vegetable oil, such as sunflower, sesame or other flavourless oil

Wash and partly peel the aubergine by peeling off strips to create a striped effect. Split into two lengthways, then cut each half into four sticks. Cut the sticks into irregular smaller pieces.

Wash the yuzu, zest the peel and squeeze out the juice. Mix 2 teaspoons of the juice with everything but the aubergine and yuzu zest.

In a frying pan (skillet), heat a generous amount of oil over a medium heat, then fry the aubergine until it starts to soften. Lower the temperature and add the miso mixture. Taste to see if any additional sweetness, acidity or saltiness is needed. When the aubergine is soft, remove from heat, put into a bowl and sprinkle with some yuzu zest.

This dish can be eaten when it has cooled, but if you've stored it in the refrigerator, I'd heat it up. If you can't get hold of fresh yuzu, bottled juice works just as well.

It can be silky smooth, firm, chewy, deep-fried, sweet, hot or cold, eaten raw or cooked. Just as the miso soup is a subject for debate and sometimes disagreement, so is tofu. However, this delightful food has been greatly misunderstood. Made from soy beans that are first turned into soy milk and then curdled, tofu is packed with protein and can be served in a range of different ways. Of course, how and where the tofu is made impacts the flavour. The better the water, the better the tofu. Kyoto's great water has made them famous for their white blocks of tofu for this very reason. I remember biking around the small back streets of the city early one autumn (fall) morning and passing a tiny, ancient tofu store. An old man was packaging the morning's batch while people from the neighbourhood were walking by, getting their daily piece of incredibly fresh tofu. It was like a scene out of a movie that I wanted to be part of.

Kyoto is also home to one of my all-time best food memories. It's from a *ryokan* – a traditional Japanese inn – in the mountains south of the city, where an acquaintance of mine and his wife serve a very unique *kaiseki* menu, a traditional Japanese meal consisting of up to 14 dishes made from locally sourced ingredients. It is an experience that leaves nothing to chance. The food served for dinner is incredible in so many ways, but the breakfast beat everything I've had in my life so far. The freshly-made tofu – scooped up warm and served with a simple dashi – still flashes through my memory from time to time. Not complicated but perfectly balanced between soft sweetness and savoury.

Tofu

Yudofu

As I have mentioned, Kyoto is famous for tofu and ever since I first visited the city I've been going to a *yudofu* (boiled tofu) restaurant in the eastern mountains, a place where they serve nothing but a set meal of Zen-Buddhist tofu cuisine. Their main dish is a large ceramic pot of steaming hot tofu, served with spring onions (scallions) and a warm sauce – a culinary delight, made even better when eaten while sitting on tatami mats between sliding doors. Sometimes you feel in the mood for something light and healthy – or you haven't got the time or energy to cook much at all. Then, this might just be your go-to: simply get a block of tofu and you're good to go.

Serves 4

TOFU
2 × 4 cm (1½ in) piece of konbu (optional)
300 g (10½ oz) firm tofu, drained and cut into 4 pieces
1–2 spring onions (scallions), thinly sliced
shichimi (optional)

DASHI
200 ml (7 fl oz/scant 1 cup) water
2 teaspoons dashi powder
6 tablespoons soy sauce
4 teaspoons sake

To cook the tofu, bring a saucepan of water and the *konbu,* if using, to a gentle boil. Lower the tofu into the water using a perforated ladle until it is completely submerged and let it boil for about 6 minutes.

While the tofu is cooking, in another pan, combine the water, dashi powder, soy sauce and sake over a medium heat.

Carefully, lift out the tofu with a perforated ladle and put into bowls, then top with the spring onions before pouring the warm dashi over the top. Sprinkle with shichimi, if using (I highly recommend it!).

Tofu & sesame salad

This dish was a regular on the table at my former Japanese host family's house. Maybe Yukiyo, my host mother, kept making it because she realised how much I liked it – I love tofu, sesame and most things that are a little sweet. It's a simple little dish that isn't too demanding either in preparation or in flavour.

Serves 4

200 g (7 oz) baby spinach, rinsed
3 teaspoons irigoma, or toasted sesame seeds
200 g (7 oz) silken tofu
2 tablespoons mirin
1½ teaspoons soy sauce or 2 teaspoons light soy sauce
⅓ teaspoon sugar

Bring a large saucepan of water to the boil. Blanch the spinach in the boiling water for 40–60 seconds, then immediately lift out and rinse under cold running water. When completely cool, use your hands to squeeze out any excess water, then set aside.

Reserve a few of the *irigoma*, then use a pestle and mortar to lightly grind the rest.

Put all the ingredients except the spinach and reserved *irigoma* into a bowl and mix together until smooth. Separate the spinach from each other and fold into the tofu mixture. Sprinkle with the last of the *irigoma*.

This is best served at room temperature. It keeps for a day or two in the refrigerator.

This dish should not be very salty, so rather underdo than overdo the soy sauce, and serve it with another slightly salty dish to make a nice contrast.

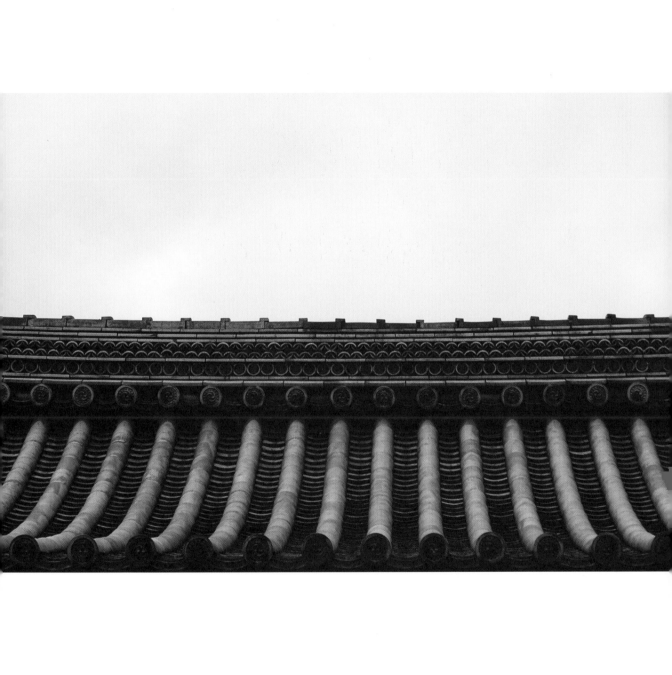

Creamy tofu, mushroom & Jerusalem artichoke

There is a small modern restaurant close to Heian Shrine in Kyoto, a place with stunning architecture by Toshihito Yokouchi. You enter what feels like an exquisite home, with room for ten people around the dining table and an upstairs coffee/living room with windows overlooking a small stream. They serve a modern Japanese breakfast by a communal table where, in an untraditional way, for Japan, the food is placed on large plates in the middle for everyone to share. In one of those beautiful ceramic bowls, I encountered something similar to this white, creamy composition, which is a perfect combination of two great things: tofu and cream cheese. It lifted tofu to new heights and I probably had three helpings. This recipe is what I ended up with when trying to recreate that experience.

Serves 4

3 medium-sized Jerusalem artichokes, about 190 g (6½ oz)
300 g (10½ oz) mixed mushrooms (such as portobello, enoki, oyster, shiitake)
sunflower or rapeseed (canola) oil
300 g (10½ oz) silken tofu
100 g (3½ oz) cream cheese
1½ tablespoons mirin
1 teaspoon soy sauce (preferably light)
1 teaspoon sugar (optional)
sea salt
a pinch of dashi powder, to garnish

Wash the Jerusalem artichokes and, keeping the peel on, cut into thin 2 mm (1/16 in) slices. Bring a large saucepan of salted water to the boil, then blanch the chokes for 1–2 minutes. Lift out of the water and immediately rinse under cold running water until cool. Set aside to drain in a strainer.

Brush any dirt from the mushrooms, then cut them into thin 2–3 mm (⅛ in) slices. If you have small mushrooms or enoki, adjust the size accordingly, or leave them whole, as you don't want the pieces too small.

Heat a frying pan (skillet) with a little oil, then fry the mushrooms over a medium–high heat until golden. Add a pinch or two of salt during the process. Transfer to a plate and leave to cool.

In a bowl, combine everything except the vegetables and whisk until completely smooth. Then fold in the cooled mushrooms and Jerusalem artichokes. Top with a pinch of dashi powder.

Even though Japan serves up some very delicious meat dishes, my love affair with the cuisine has always been on the sea side of things. Fatty, grilled mackerel. Salty salmon. Flaky cod. Slices of thick sashimi. Salmon roe. The plethora of treasures from the sea never lets you down and if one were to try to write about it all that would require no less than an *Odyssey*. Here are just a few dishes that are frequent favourites in my kitchen and that don't require years of training before you master them.

Fish

Sweet miso cod

I haven't met anyone who doesn't appreciate this dish. Flaky pieces of white fish finished off with a sweet, umami miso flavour. Variations are served here and there at restaurants both in Japan and around the world, so I wouldn't claim the idea of it is mine, but whomever thought of this combination in the first place was a genius. I prefer to make the marinade with *nigori* (less filtered) sake, which is a little sweeter than regular and, by cutting the fish before marinating it, you allow for the sake flavour to really soak in. I like to use cod backs, but a thick cod fillet would be fine. If you can get hold of *skrei*, it is super-delicious – a Norwegian cod that swims upstream to mate, thus becoming larger, with very white, firm but flaky meat.

Serves 4

500 g (1 lb 2 oz) cod backs,
cod fillet or skrei
4 tablespoons white miso
4 tablespoons mirin
2 teaspoons sake (nigori)
2 teaspoons sugar

THE DAY BEFORE SERVING

Cut the fish into portion-sized pieces and put into a ziplock bag. Mix the miso, mirin, sake and sugar. Pour the mixture over the fish and massage until all pieces are covered with marinade. Leave to rest in the refrigerator overnight.

THE DAY OF SERVING

Take the fish out of the refrigerator and leave it to come back to room temperature while you preheat the oven to 180°C (350°F/gas 4) and line a baking pan with baking parchment. Pat the fish dry with paper towels to remove any excess miso, then put it in the prepared baking pan and bake in the upper part of the oven for about 5–10 minutes until the fish flakes easily. The time will depend on the thickness of the slices. Serve the dish warm or cool.

If you can get hold of very fresh cod, the end result will be even better if you let the fish marinate for two days. And if you have a charcoal grill at hand why not bring it out?

Pickled herring & cucumber sesame salad

Pickled herring is not really what you'd find at the Japanese table, I admit. However, it's one of those Swedish flavours, similar to some of the dishes I've come across in Japan – in particular, the marinated mackerel *shime saba*. I found that herring goes so well with other parts of the classic Japanese cuisine, too. This small salad tastes just as good served with rice as it does with new potatoes.

Serves 4

½ cucumber
100 g (3½ oz) pickled herring, preferably unflavoured or onion-flavoured, or you can substitute with shime saba
1 tablespoon irigoma, or toasted sesame seeds

Wash the cucumber and slice into 1 mm (1/32 in) slices using a mandoline. Cut the herring into 1 cm (½ in) pieces. Reserve a little of the *irigoma* for garnish, then roughly grind the rest using a pestle and mortar. Mix all the ingredients in a bowl and divide into portions to serve, sprinkling with the reserved *irigoma*.

If you have time then let the salad rest for 10–20 minutes to allow the cucumber to start releasing liquid, making the whole thing deliciously juicy.

Asparagus & ikura

Even though we eat quite a substantial amount of salmon in Sweden, the roe is not something you'd come in contact with very often. In Japan, it is known as *ikura* and you often find it both on sushi and or as part of a *donburi* – a bed of rice covered in heaps of the small orange spheres. I love how they pop in your mouth! They are both fun to eat and beautiful to look at. This combination is a buttery, smoky sensation with the crisp asparagus as a pleasing contrast.

Serves 4

8 asparagus stems
1 spring onion (scallion)
3–4 tablespoons salmon roe
a dash of soy sauce
a pinch of bonito flakes
vegetable oil, for frying

Start by cleaning the asparagus and breaking off the bottom of the stems to get rid of the woody parts – if you try bending them close to the root they will easily snap off at the right place. Cut or break each stem into three pieces and set aside. Wash the spring onion and cut into 2 cm (¾ in) pieces, cutting into shorter pieces as you get closer to the root.

Heat a frying pan (skillet) over a medium–high heat, add a dash of oil and then add the asparagus. Swirl the pan while you fry the pieces for about 2 minutes, making sure they do not burn. Add the spring onion and fry together until the asparagus turns lightly golden but still has a little bite. It should still be firm but without a raw core.

Spoon the vegetables onto plates, add a spoonful of salmon roe, a dash of soy sauce and a pinch of bonito flakes on top. Et voilà.

If you want to add another dimension of smokiness, the asparagus can also be charcoal barbecued and the spring onion fried separately.

Pasta was my absolute favourite food when I was growing up. Any shape or form; any day of the week. Had it been up to me, we would have eaten pasta on a daily basis, preferably the homemade, fresh one my dad and I made together from time to time (I still do make a mean carbonara). No wonder I fell immediately and hard for the Japanese noodles: soba, udon, ramen, somen, nyuumen… Cold in the summer, warm in the winter.

A bowl of salty noodles is uncomplicated in both flavour and preparation. Great to lift a hangover and sometimes an instant ramen is exactly what you need and and about all you can manage after a long day at work. If you don't decide to embark on the journey of actually making the noodles yourself (which is a lengthy business), the following recipes are really just as easy as throwing together the simplest of pasta dishes.

Noodles

Somen

Of all the Japanese-style noodles, the thin, white, wheat somen are my favourite. There's something about their saltiness and their thinner-than-spaghetti shape that makes them a delight to eat. When eaten in the summer they are called *somen* and served on ice with a dipping sauce, *tsuyu*, on the side. It's usually made with freshly grated ginger and spring onions (scallions), but I prefer mine with wasabi and shiso.

Serves 4

TSUYU
75–100 ml (2½–3½ fl oz/ about ⅓ cup) sake
1½ teaspoons dashi powder
150 ml (5 fl oz/scant ⅔ cup) dark soy sauce
150 ml (5 fl oz/scant ⅔ cup) mirin
300 ml (10 fl oz/1¼ cups) cold water

NOODLES
400 g (14 oz) somen
salt
ice

TO SERVE
4 shiso leaves, washed and thinly sliced
wasabi

Start by making the *tsuyu* as this needs time to cool. Bring the sake to the boil in a large saucepan and simmer for a few seconds to vaporise the alcohol, then add all the remaining *tsuyu* ingredients except the water. Simmer for 5 minutes. Add the cold water and set aside to cool.

Divide the shiso and wasabi among four small dishes.

Bring a large saucepan of salted water to the boil. Cook the noodles for 2½–3 minutes, depending on how al dente you want them. Once cooked to your liking, rinse immediately in cold water until cool. Plate the noodles on top of a layer of ice and serve with individual small bowls of *tsuyu*.

When eating, add the shiso and wasabi onion to the cold *tsuyu*, pick up some noodles and dip before indulging.

Nyuumen

During the cold season in Japan, somen are usually put into a hot soup instead of being served with a cold dipping sauce, and they are then referred to as *nyuumen*. The first time I tried them was a during winter almost ten years ago when visiting a temple somewhere in the Kansai area. Close to the entrance was a very small noodle shop run by two elderly ladies. I'm not even sure we were hungry but it felt almost mandatory to have a portion each, and I'm glad we did. In ceramic bowls of appetising size came these thin, but not too soft, noodles in a broth that I could have kept drinking all day. I can't recall what toppings they came with because the noodles stole the show, but I sometimes top mine with a poached egg and fresh mizuna or similar green leaves. It's hard to say if hot is better than cold, but they are equally easy to prepare.

Serves 4

DASHI
1.6 litres (54 fl oz/6¾ cups) water
6 teaspoons dashi powder
8 tablespoons soy sauce
4 tablespoons mirin

NOODLES
400 g (14 oz) somen
sea salt

TO SERVE
2 spring onions (scallions), thinly sliced
shichimi, optional

Start by making the dashi. Combine all the dashi ingredients in a saucepan and bring to the boil, then reduce the heat while you cook the noodles.

Bring a large saucepan of water to the boil with a pinch of salt. Add the noodles and simmer for 2½ minutes (or according to the packet instructions) until al dente. Drain, rinse in cool water, then pour into serving bowls, pour over the hot dashi and top with the spring onions and a sprinkling of *shichimi*.

Green somen salad

This came about in one of those classic moments when you only have random, leftovers in the refrigerator that was not meant to go together. Then you go out on a limb, put them together, add some garlic and magic happens. It is that kind of dish.

Serves 2

DRESSING
1 large garlic clove, peeled
and lightly squashed
4 tablespoons olive oil, plus extra
for frying
3 tablespoons soy sauce
3 tablespoons grain vinegar
1½ tablespoons mirin

NOODLES
200 g (14 oz) somen

VEGETABLES
2 handfuls of fresh crispy greens (such as
mizuna or watercress), washed
1 fennel bulb, thinly sliced
1 avocado, cut into slices
2 teaspoons grated horseradish
a few springs of dill, chopped

TO SERVE
a few sprigs of dill
zest of ½ lemon

To make the dressing, heat a small pan over a medium heat, add a generous dash of olive oil and then add the garlic clove. Fry until creamy all the way through, stirring continuously to make sure it doesn't burn. Remove the garlic from the pan and leave to cool a little before chopping finely. Mix the fried, chopped garlic with the soy sauce, vinegar, mirin and olive oil into a dressing. Set aside.

Meanwhile, bring a large pan of water to the boil, add the noodles and cook for 2½ minutes, then immediately drain and rinse in cold water until cool.

Mix the noodles, green leaves, fennel, horseradish, chopped dill and dressing, then carefully tuck in the avocado slices. Top with dill springs and lemon zest.

Udon with poached egg & fish roe

Until recently, udon noodles were not a favourite of mine. But over the past few years, I've grown to like this thicker wheat noodle more and more. What finally won me over was the uncomplicated 600-yen bowl I had on the small island of Naoshima. Perfectly chewy, freshly-made noodles in a simple broth. Nothing more, nothing less, but it brought such satisfaction.

This recipe requires a little more effort, perhaps because that's what's needed when you don't have a 70-year-old grandmother cutting noodles in your kitchen. It has both fresh greens and a small amount of soup, along with both eggs and fish roe, neatly plated and then mixed together.

Serves 2

NOODLES
1 small silver onion
200 g (7 oz) udon noodles
2 handfuls of mizuna or watercress
2–4 tablespoons lumpfish or salmon roe
1 sheet of nori, cut into thin strips,
or 4 large pinches of pre-cut nori

EGGS
2 eggs
1 tablespoon apple cider or
white wine vinegar

SAUCE
300 ml (10 fl oz/1¼ cups) water
⅓ teaspoon dashi powder
1 tablespoon sake
3 tablespoons mirin
4 tablespoons soy sauce
2–3 teaspoons yuzu juice

Start by slicing the onion thinly using a mandoline or a very sharp knife. Put it into a bowl, cover with cold water and set aside. Prepare the eggs by cracking each into a small bowl.

Make the sauce by combining the water, dashi powder, sake, mirin and soy sauce in a saucepan. Bring slowly to a gentle boil, then turn off the heat. Add the yuzu juice and taste for saltiness, adding more soy sauce or dashi if needed. Keep warm, or reheat gently when ready to serve.

To poach the eggs, put about 5 cm (2 in) of water in a large saucepan and bring to the boil, add the vinegar and lower to a gentle simmer. Swirl the water with a spoon until a small vortex is created, then pour 1 egg into the middle and let it simmer gently for 1 minute 45 seconds before lifting it out with a slotted spoon. Repeat with the second egg.

Meanwhile, bring a large pan of salted water to the boil, add the noodles and cook according to the instructions until al dente (dried noodles takes about 6–8 minutes). Drain, then rinse once. Spoon the noodles into serving bowls and top with the greens, roe, the egg and nori. Finish by pouring over the warm sauce.

When eating, split the egg so that the runny yolk mixes with the sauce and noodles.

Upon first arriving in Japan, I was surprised by the fact that desserts were not a particularly big thing. The most common item to finish off a meal is fruit. But, being Japan, it was not just any old fruit, but a piece of perfect melon or a strawberry tasting as though it had been literally soaking in sun. So who am I to complain? Don't get me wrong, there are, of course, Japanese sweets and snacks, it was just that they were in a shape and form so unfamiliar to my senses. Rice and beans didn't really scream dessert to me, even with added sugar. A few years down the road, I now from time to time crave a piece of good *yokan* – a sweet bean jelly – or a beautiful *wagashi* – Japanese plant-based confectionery – to accompany my matcha. Since learning to cook proper *anko* – a red bean and sugar paste – takes a lifetime (or so they say) and *ohagi* – an *anko*-covered rice ball – is an acquired taste, the sweets I have included here, inspired by more modern flavours I've met in different places, are hopefully a little more accessible.

Sweet

Date & walnut wagashi

Wagashi are typically exquisitely beautiful sweets made from various plants and sugar, to be served with green tea. Even though they come in an endless number of versions, many tend to be demanding on a foreign palate. This little treat, on the other hand, has found favour with everyone who has tried it. It is a version of a modern *wagashi* that I've come across, where the sweet, salt, fat and nuts blend together beautifully, creating almost a caramel-like flavour. It is a perfect end to a meal, especially as a side to the somewhat bitter matcha.

Serves 4

4 small or medium walnuts
about 4 teaspoons salted butter
4 medjool dates
sea salt

Preheat the oven to 180°C (350°F/gas 4). Take the butter out of the refrigerator to allow it to come to room temperature and soften a bit.

Spread the walnuts in a roasting pan and toast in the oven for about 7–8 minutes, or until fragrant. Take out and leave to cool.

With a sharp knife, cut open the dates lengthways on one side and pick out the pit. Fill one side of the date with butter using a butter knife, then sprinkle with a little sea salt. Place a whole walnut on top of the butter and carefully 'close' the other half of the date around the walnut so that it is more or less covered. Serve at room temperature. The *wagashi* will keep in the refrigerator for at least two days.

Make sure you choose whole walnuts that are small or medium sized as you want to be able to fit the whole walnut inside the dates. Take the time to toast the nuts since this removes the bitterness, which can otherwise take over.

Nashi & melon

As I mentioned, fruit is a very common dessert and something we would have after dinner more or less every day when I lived in Kaizuka: carefully peeled sweet apple wedges, a tart *hassaku* orange that made your tongue curl, or plump and juicy red grapes. When in season, we would even have *mikan* from the back yard. So even if this might not count as a recipe, not including fruit here wouldn't be fair to reality.

If you haven't come across it before, *nashi*, or a Japanese/Chinese pear, is a really crispy fruit with loads of juiciness, like a mix between a pear and a water chestnut. It is incredibly refreshing and a perfect way to finish off a meal. If nashi proves hard to find, you could also use a Kaiser (Bose) pear as long as it is a little on the firm and tart side.

Serves 4

1 nashi
1 small honeydew melon
zest of 1 lemon

Peel the nashi and melon and cut into wedges. Arrange on a plate and top with lemon zest.

Almond-milk pudding

In Japan, pudding, or *purin*, is a popular sweet snack or dessert. One of my favourites is the very smooth but oh-so-simple Morinaga Milk Pudding, which you can find from time to time in convenience stores or supermarkets (I'm always on the hunt). This dessert is really a combination of that smoothness and my gravitation to anything tasting of almonds. The recipe came about on a recent trip to Tokyo, when I was recommended to have lunch at a small udon restaurant in the Naka-Meguro neighbourhood; a place filled with quirky books and where the hand-cut noodles were some of the best I've had in the city. The meal ended perfectly with a small bowl of *annin* tofu, a traditionally Chinese pudding made from apricot kernel milk, soft and with a distinct bitter almond flavour. When I started to write this book, I decided to try combining the milky notes and smooth texture of the milk pudding with the almond in the annin tofu to make an almond-flavoured milk pudding-ish dessert. It turned out to be a pudding not dissimilar to panna cotta – like eating milky, almond clouds.

Serves 4–6

2 gelatine sheets
200 ml (7 fl oz/scant 1 cup) milk
200 ml (7 fl oz/scant 1 cup) double (heavy) cream
2½ tablespoons sugar
5 drops bitter almond essence
a handful of toasted almonds, to serve

Soak the gelatine sheets in cold water for at least 5 minutes.

Combine all the remaining ingredients in a saucepan and heat up gently. When steaming hot, turn off the heat. Pour the soaking water off the gelatine and mix the soaked gelatine sheets into the mixture until completely melted. Let the mixture cool down for about 30 minutes, then then give it a stir and divide among four or six small bowls or glasses. Leave to rest in the refrigerator for another 4–6 hours.

Serve topped with toasted almonds.

I could write a whole book on tea alone. The subtle flavours. The rituals around it. The changes in colours. The vessels holding this magic liquid. Because it is magic – how it calms all your senses, both in the practice of brewing it as well as in the moment of drinking.

In Japanese, the word for tea is *cha* (茶). However, when speaking about tea in general the honorific prefix 'o' is always added: *ocha*. It is a way of showing respect to the object and demonstrates the homage paid to this drink. And there's no better way to start or end a day.

Tea

The leaves

There is a range of different Japanese teas, as well as ways of preparing hot and cold drinks from the leaves. The general term for Japanese green tea is *ryokucha*. What distinguishes *ryokucha* from black tea is that the leaves have not gone through fermentation, but are steamed directly after harvest – keeping that fresh green colour alive. On the following pages, you will find a few common variations that are on constant rotation on my table (and at any given time during the day).

Store your leaves in an airtight container in the refrigerator. This way they stay fresh and keep their flavour for longer.

Sencha

Sencha (煎茶) is the all-time, everyday drink. It's what's being sipped on a daily basis, both with and in between meals. As with all *ryokucha,* the leaves are not fermented but steamed fresh for about 15–20 seconds before being rolled and dried, to prevent oxidation. This way of preparing the leaves also creates the distinctive green colour with yellow tones of the brewed *sencha.*

Grassy and sometimes seaweedy notes are usually prominent, but the flavour varies with water temperatures and the quality of the leaves.

Sencha *is usually prepared at around 75–80°C (167–176°F) and steeped for about 40 seconds or up to 1½ minutes, depending on how strong a flavour you are looking for. I usually let it steep on the longer side when serving with food, using 1 teaspoon of the leaves to 50 ml (3 tablespoons) of water. In the summer, I cold-brew it by putting 4 teaspoons of leaves into 1 litre (34 fl oz/4 cups) of cold water and letting it steep for an hour before straining and placing in the refrigerator.*

Genmaicha

Genmaicha (玄米茶), *sencha* with roasted brown rice, is best described as a bright green tea with grassy notes and a popcorn flavour, which is from the roasted rice (sometimes rice grains even end up 'popping' during the roasting process – very cute). It is a fairly easy tea on the palate, making it a great introduction to the world of *ryokucha* if you are new to Japanese tea. There are also variants where matcha is included in the blend, *matcha-iri genmaicha*, resulting in very high intensity in both flavour and colour, perfect to go alongside a sweet treat.

I drink *genmaicha* both with food and stand-alone (then again, I always drink tea...), but in my opinion it serves better as a complement to food with softer flavours, such as Zosui (page 26) or Somen (page 107).

Genmaicha *is usually prepared at around 80–85°C (176–185°F) and, in my opinion, is best steeped for 1–2 minutes, depending on the desired intensity. Some say up to 2 g (2 teaspoons) of leaves per 50 ml (3 tablespoons) of water, but I prefer my tea on the lighter side, so most often I use 1 teaspoon of leaves per 50 ml (3 tablespoons) of water. I like to use an unglazed pot for this tea, one specifically assigned to popcorn flavours, that is.*

Hojicha

Hojicha (保持茶) is one of those teas that has yet to become commonly served outside of Japan. First invented by tea merchants in the 1920s in Kyoto, it is an innovation that sprung from trying to put across a lower-grade product at a premium price. They started charcoal-roasting the green tea leaves and ended up with a reddish-brown, smooth tea with a nutty aroma and no sharpness, both thirst-quenching and comforting. Though the cheaper *bancha* (normal tea) are the most common leaves used for *hojicha*, both *kukicha* (a tea blend made of stems, stalks, and twigs) or low-grade *sencha* can be used. Another upside to this tea is that roasting the leaves reduces the caffeine level, and so *hojicha* is perfect for finishing off a meal or drinking later in the evening.

Hojicha is usually prepared at around 85–95°C (185–203°F) and steeped for between 30 seconds up to 3 minutes. The longer you steep, the darker the colour and the more intense the flavour. I normally land between 1–2 minutes. Glazed or glass teaware is recommended, otherwise the strong flavour from the roasting can be soaked up by unglazed areas. Since this is a favourite tea of mine, I have a special pot assigned to making it.

Matcha

There has been a lot of hype surrounding matcha (抹茶) around the world, partly through the spread of the sweet, light green matcha latte, and greatly thanks to the tea's so-called superfood qualities. The traditional Japanese matcha, on the other hand, is an intensely green, mostly bitter drink with no added sugar, dating back to the 12th century. It is prepared by whisking together a powder of finely ground tea leaves with warm water until foamy, which is then served in exquisitely designed ceramic bowls, *matcha chawan*, with a sweet *Wagashi* (see page 107) on the side.

To make matcha, tea leaves that have been protected from direct sunlight, known as *tencha*, are ground into a very fine powder using a stone mill. The powder is then carefully prepared with water and a *chasen*, a bamboo whisk, to create a light froth. The preparation of matcha is an art in itself and getting to that perfect froth is not as easy as it might look. Taking classes in this art of whisking is not uncommon even amongst the Japanese. However, the effort required is to me part of the enjoyment of the drink, imposing a ritual which is completed with that last sip of bitter-sweet green.

chawan or bowl
chasen (bamboo whisk)
1–2 teaspoons matcha
75 ml (2½ fl oz/⅓ cup) hot water at 80°C (176°C)

Fill the bowl with hot water to heat it, then dry with a towel. Sift the matcha through a sieve into the bowl. Pour over the water and whisk vigorously until frothy. Serve immediately with something sweet, such as Wagashi *(page 120) or a small piece of chocolate. The higher the quality of tea, the easier it will be to get that frothy drink with sweet notes. You will need to use a bowl as a cup or mug won't allow for whisking.*

The vessels

My older sister often asks me – over a cup of *sencha* or *hojicha* – what I do differently when preparing my tea, puzzled as to why she doesn't feel she reaches the same flavour even though she is using the same leaves. Of course, it depends on the leaves, water temperature and steeping time. However, something which impacts the end result immensely is the vessel you brew and serve it in. Tea is not solely about the flavour – it is just as much a visual and emotional experience, similar to the appreciation of a piece of art.

In order to avoid tea that cools too quickly, I usually warm up the kyuusu *and* yunomi *(teapot and serving bowl) by filling them with hot water. It is also a way to cool the brewing water to the right temperature; you can then use the water from the cups to steep the tea by pouring it over the leaves.*

Kyuusu

Setting matcha apart, the *ryokucha* leaves should be brewed in a pot that allows them to float around freely. In Japan, the teapot commonly used is a *kyuusu* (急須) with either a handle on the side or over the top. These pots have a built-in mesh-like strainer on the inside, allowing room for the leaves to fully unfold. Collecting the leaves in a small or tight sieve will prevent them from expanding properly and thus impede the infusion of flavours.

Secondly, size matters. Since *ryokucha* should be consumed as soon as it has been steeped to maintain the best flavour, the size of the pot should be adjusted to how many people you are brewing for, and, of course, the size of the cup you use. Keeping the leaves in the water for too long will make the tea bitter, so when pouring you should be able to empty the pot completely.

Another thing to remember, especially when using ceramic teapots, is not to use the same pot for different tea leaves. For instance, I use different pots for *sencha* and *hojicha* since the pot, if not glazed or glass, will soak up flavour from the tea and vice versa. Thus, over time your pot will become impregnated with flavours (which is a good thing!), and you don't want to disturb a new brewing with flavours from a whole other sort of tea. The Earl Grey-*sencha* mix defeats the purpose either way.

Yunomi

Going back to serving tea to my sisters, they have repeatedly laughed at me over the years when I have brought home one small-sized tea cup after another. Questioning the need for such a range of cups and, in their eyes, their miniature size. But, for me, there is an important point to this, because the cup, the *yunomi* (湯呑み) is central to the drinking experience.

As I mentioned earlier, *ryokucha* should be consumed shortly after brewing since the flavours keep changing with time and temperature, just like any good wine. The ideal size of a *yunomi* is 90–160 ml (3–5½ fl oz/ ⅓–¾ cup), preferably in a colour and finish that allows you to appreciate the colour of the tea. Just as the size and colour is important, so is the shape and thickness. I usually prefer a thinner cup as this presents the subtle flavours in a beautiful way and is easy on the lips. So, instead of having one large cup, try brewing the leaves several times and relish many small ones.

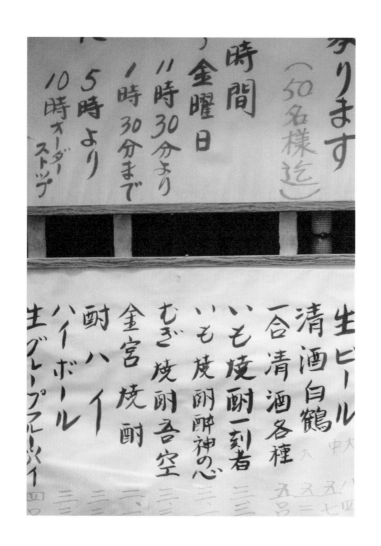

あります（50名様迄）

時間
金曜日
11時30分より
1時30分まで
5時より
10時オーダーストップ

生ビール　大中小
清酒白鶴
一合清酒各種
いも焼酎一刻者
いも焼酎酔神の心
むぎ焼酎吾空
金宮焼酎
酎ハイ
ハイボール
生グレープフルーツハイ

As I mentioned early on in the book, most of these dishes, with a few exceptions, are not stand-alone but are meant to be combined with each other. One, two or three side dishes, a soup, some pickles and rice. Play around and try out a few variations, or choose one of the following combinations that I find go well together. And I hardly need to say: don't forget the tea.

As for setting the table: chopsticks go parallel and close to the table edge, miso soup to the right, rice to the left and the main dish somewhere above; *tsukemono* goes adjacent to the rice and the remaining dishes above the main dish. Roughly. I could preach about exact placement, but as long as you are comfortable eating, I dare say it doesn't really matter (at least on my table). The only thing I would stay completely away from is pouring soy sauce on your rice – it's like drenching a proper carbonara in ketchup. Also, the stickiness keeping the rice grains together will be destroyed, which will put you in a tight spot with the chopsticks. Let the umami in the side dishes and soup add the saltiness to balance with your rice.

When you're getting ready to eat, start with plating the side dishes and *tsukemono* as these do not have to be steaming hot, then serve the warm rice and hot soup, adjusting the amount to how hungry you are. In Japan, generally speaking, the more food you need, the larger your rice bowl will be. Though I could never compete with the amount of rice that goes into any teenage boy, I will happily eat two servings after a workout.

On the table

The main purpose of the *utsuwa*, the vessel, is not only to hold the food but to heighten the eating experience, enhancing the food it is holding. Not surprisingly, in Japan great attention is paid to the combination of food and container or plate on which it is presented. I have never enjoyed anywhere else the full sensory eating experiences I've had in Japan: times when it seemed as though the plate had been made for the specific dish it was carrying, when your eyes just couldn't take it all in.

In many Japanese homes, every family member has their personal rice bowl (*chawan*) and chopsticks (*ohashi*), chosen to suit the size of their hands, mouth and stomach, as well as in a design to suit their taste. People don't own ten plates of the same design, but a few selected pieces, which have been chosen with care and affection.

Recently my friend Maya taught me why many Japanese people don't seem to use their dishwasher regularly, even though they own one. Washing a bowl or plate by hand is a way of showing appreciation for its beauty and deepens your relationship with that piece. In such a way, the affection will grow over time, and the vessel becomes more than a simple tool for carrying food. I tend to take a few moments to contemplate which plate or bowl to use to serve a dish, even if I am eating alone. It can turn an otherwise plain meal into a moment of joy. It also gives you a reason to start cherishing those moments by the sink.

Tofu & sesame salad (page 84)
Genmaicha (page 137)
Ginger-pickled Chinese leaf (page 55)
Simple miso soup with shiitake & spring onion (page 35)
Gohan (page 22) served with salmon roe & shiso

Soy-pickled eggs (page 61)
Somen (page 107)
Greens, as you please

Sweet miso cod (page 95)
Clear shiitake soup (page 38)
Shiso- & salt-pickled cucumber (page 50)
Gohan (page 22)

Gohan (page 22)
Simple miso soup with tofu, spring onion
* & wakame (page 35)*
Soy-pickled eggs (page 61)

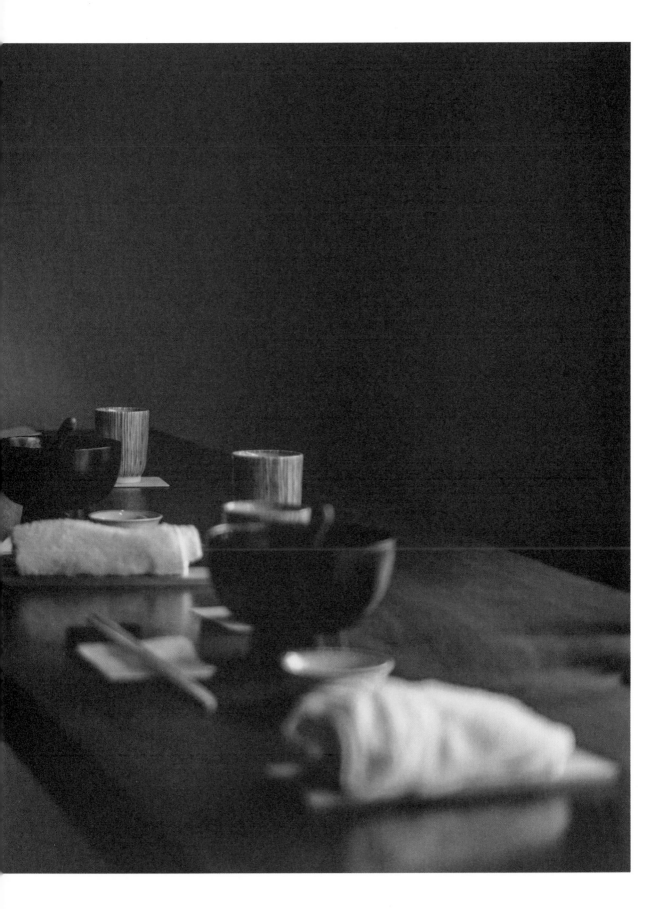

There are a number of people who have been part of bringing this book to life, to you all goes my sincerest gratitude.

Yukiyo Sugioka
Lovisa Hellsten
Victoria Hellsten
Catrine Isehed
Lasse Hellsten
Natalie de Brun
Isabelle Skaräng
Maya Matsuura
Akemi Matsuura
Christofer Geijer
Jonna Jess
Kate Pollard
Eila Purvis
Grönska Stadsodling
Alma

Acknowledgements

Sofia Hellsten is a food and travel photographer and writer, with a background within communication and business strategy. She's also the woman behind the Stockholm Japanese brunch experience, *Leaves & Grains*.

Although born in Sweden, Sofia has been savouring the Japanese kitchen over the past 11 years, ever since first living in the country back in 2008. When not exploring Japan, you'll find her in her tiny Stockholm kitchen prepping brunch, drinking tea or pickling greens. You can best keep up with her on Instagram @shellsten or www.s-hellsten.com

About the Author

心からありがとうございます。

Index

Published in 2019 by Hardie Grant Books, an imprint of Hardie Grant Publishing

Hardie Grant Books (London)
5th & 6th Floors
52–54 Southwark Street
London SE1 1UN

Hardie Grant Books (Melbourne)
Building 1, 658 Church Street
Richmond, Victoria 3121

hardiegrantbooks.com

British Library Cataloguing-in-Publication Data. A catalogue record for this book
is available from the British Library.

The Japanese Table by Sofia Hellsten
ISBN: 978-1-78488-215-0

Publishing Director: Kate Pollard
Junior Editor: Eila Purvis
Designer and photographer: Sofia Hellsten
Copy Editor: Wendy Hobson
Proofreader: Emily Preece-Morrison
Indexer: Cathy Heath

Colour Reproduction by p2d
Printed and bound in China by Leo Paper Group